ENGLAND
of One Hundred Years Ago
PHOTOGRAPH COLLECTION

NORTH WILTSHIRE

SELECTED BY DAVID BUXTON

ALAN SUTTON

First published in the United Kingdom in 1992
by Alan Sutton Publishing Limited
Phoenix Mill, Stroud, Gloucestershire

First published in the United States of America
by Alan Sutton Publishing Incorporated
83 Washington Avenue, Dover, New Hampshire

British Library and Library of Congress
Cataloguing in Publication Data applied for

ISBN 0-7509-0304-X

Typesetting and origination by
Alan Sutton Publishing Limited
Graphics and Design Department.
Printed in Great Britain by
Bath Colour Books.

Some blemishes have been removed by extreme enlargement of the image to individual pixel
level, with careful computer graphics surgery to mend scratches, foxing, or other damage to the
photographic image.

ENGLAND
of One Hundred Years Ago
VOLUME SIX

North Wiltshire

The photograph collection of England of One Hundred Years Ago is an attempt to find and produce some of the best images in existence from late Victorian times up to the onset of the First World War. The country has been split into the traditional counties and this volume, numbered 6, represents North Wiltshire.

The criteria for selection are quality and clarity in the image together with subject interest. An attempt has been made to ensure a reasonable geographical balance within the area covered, but it has to be admitted that some areas were much more photographed than others.

The printed images are intended to be used for framing, although some people may wish to buy additional separate prints for framing by using the order form at the back of the book, and to keep this book intact. If the order form becomes separated from the book please write to the Phoenix Mill address advising the volume number and plate number you require.

The reproductions in this book are obtained by digital scanning and computer enhancement. Some blemishes have been removed by extreme enlargement of the image to individual pixel level, with careful computer graphics surgery to mend scratches, foxing, or other damage to the photographic image.

The pictures on the facing page show a scratch, enlarged and repaired. Some damage, or blemishes in an otherwise interesting photograph are beyond reasonable repair, and have been left.

The monochrome image is then further enhanced by being artificially separated and printed in a four colour process with a sepia bias. The result is a high quality image with visual depth. The finished printed image is then protected by a careful application of matt varnish to reduce fading and to add protection. The paper is a super-calendered, acid free, matt art of 170 grammes weight per square metre.

The contents of the photographs remain totally genuine and the enhancement and surgery are used only to mend damage and not to create artificial images!

North Wiltshire of the late nineteenth and early twentieth centuries was largely a rural area, the only exception being that of the increasingly industrial Swindon, subject of a separate volume in this series. The area was sprinkled with many small, isolated villages of thatched cottages served by a series of busy market towns, Trowbridge, Devizes and Chippenham. These photographs portray a picturesque and attractive looking period in North Wiltshire's history, although one that lacked many of the comforts of modern times.

Contents

Acknowledgements.
I should like to thank the following who have kindly allowed
us to reproduce their photographs in this publication: Market
Lavington Museum, Mr and Mrs P. Oram, Museum of English
Rural Life, Reading, Wiltshire Library and Museum Service,
Wiltshire Life Society, Peter Sheldon.

Plate 1. SCHOOL FRIENDS
Children at Malmesbury, 1896

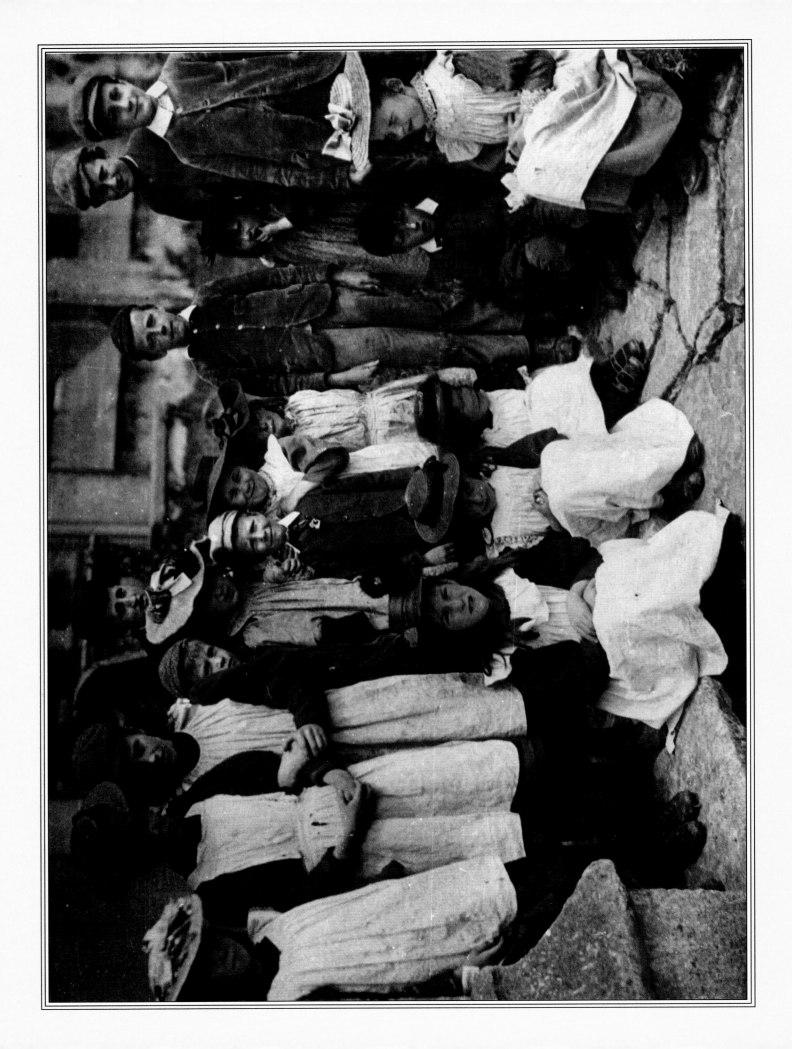

Plate 2. THE OLD TOLL-HOUSE
Shane's Castle, Devizes, *c.* 1900

Plate 3. WILTSHIRE COTTAGE
Farmworker's cottage near Coate, *c.* 1911

Plate 4. MARLBOROUGH
High Street, Marlborough, *c.* 1906

Plate 5. THE OLD OAK
High Street, Rambsbury, *c.* 1900

Plate 6. THE FINGERPOST

Old couple in Broad Hinton, *c.* 1900

Plate 7. CORSHAM

High Street, Corsham, 1906

Plate 8. THE ABBESS'S BARN
The tythe barn at Bradford on Avon, once in the ownership of the Abbess
of Shaftsbury, *c.* 1900

Plate 9. VILLAGE WEDDING

Wedding group in Avebury, *c.* 1895

Plate 10. MARKET DAY

High Steet, Wootton Bassett, *c.* 1900

Plate 11. THE MANOR KITCHEN
Kitchen interior, Avebury

Plate 12. BRATTON COTTAGERS

Old couple at Bratton, *c.*1900

Plate 13. FIRE DRILL

The fire brigade of Saxby and Farmer's engineering works, Chippenham,
1890s

Plate 14. WILTSHIRE VILLAGE

Castle Combe, *c.* 1906

Plate 15. ESCOURT FOUNTAIN
Market Place, Devizes, 1890s

Plate 16. ANCIENT STONES
Avebury, *c.* 1890

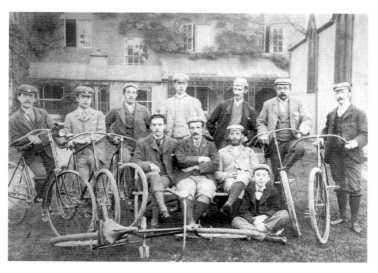

Plate 17. CHIPPENHAM WHEELERS
Chippenham Cycle Club, *c.* 1895

Plate 18. THATCHED ROOFS

Chilton Foliat, *c.* 1908

Plate 19. THE COVE

Stones at the centre of the Circle at Avebury, *c.* 1890s

Plate 20. BURDETT STREET

Ramsbury, 1907

Plate 21. THE COACHING INN

Bear Hotel and Corn Exchange, Devizes, 1898

Plate 22. FORE STREET

Trowbridge, 1900

Plate 23. VILLAGE CHILDREN
Hudswell Village, near Corsham, 1907

Plate 24. HAYMAKING

The Oram family, East End Farm, Marston, *c.* 1900

Plate 25. CHILDREN AT THE MARKET

Market Place, Devizes, 1890s

Pate 26. MEDIEVAL HOUSES

Potterne, 1898

Plate 27. BUTCHER'S CHRISTMAS

Shop of G.H.Pike, Church Street, Market Lavington, 1911

Plate 28. THE PLOUGHBOY

Ploughing near Avebury, *c.* 1900